BOYS RULE!

Contents

Matt   *Nick*

CHAPTER 1

Catch a Wave

Matt and Nick are spending a day at the beach with their families. They are in the water and Matt is teaching Nick how to body surf.

Matt "The trick is you have to start swimming with your head out of the water just before the wave breaks. Like this."

A wave approaches the boys. Matt starts thrashing his arms frantically and kicking his legs. He successfully catches the wave and rides it all the way to the beach. Moments later he swims back out to Nick.

Matt "Did you see that?"

Nick "Yes. That looked unreal!"

Matt "Okay, your turn. Here comes another one. Get ready. Now! Start kicking! Here we go!!!"

The wave rolls right over the top of Nick. Matt once again rides it all the way to shore. He swims back to Nick.

Matt "What happened? I thought you'd get that one."

Nick "Me too. I think I got most of it in my mouth. Why is sea water salty?"

Matt "Um, I don't know. Maybe there's a family of giants living up in the clouds."

Nick "What?"

Matt "Yes, and one night when they were having dinner, one of them knocked the salt pot over ... and it poured into the world's oceans."

Nick "I think the sun is frying your brain."

Matt "Wow look at this one coming! Talk about giants, this next wave is humungous! It must be three metres high."

Nick "Can I try to catch it?"

Matt "No way. It'll kill you. Even I wouldn't try to ride this one. Just dive underneath before it breaks, okay? Nick?"

Matt turns to see that Nick has already started paddling and is kicking as hard as he can.

Matt "Nick! What do you think you're doing? It's going to break you into a million pieces."

CHAPTER 2

Sand Digger

Amazingly, Nick catches the giant wave and is carried to the beach.

Nick "YAHOOOOOOO!!"

Matt swims after him.

Matt "I don't believe it! Beginner's luck! That was awesome!"

Nick "I know. I was flying. Let's do it again."

Matt "Okay, but later. I wanna have a break, now. I'm really thirsty."

Nick "Yeah, me too."

The boys run up onto the sand
and join their parents. After having
something to eat and drink, they
decide to go exploring.

Nick "Hey, look over there. Pretty
cool sandcastle, eh?"

Matt (sarcastically) "Um, *yeah*. If
you happen to be five."

Nick "What's wrong with making
sandcastles?"

Matt "Nothing—if you're playing with your little sister. Come on, let's see if we can find some dead crabs or something."

Nick "You know there's professional sandcastle makers. And they're older than us. I'll show you. I'm going to make one now."

Nick begins to dig up the beach sand and shape it into a castle. At first Matt just watches Nick, looking embarrassed, but then he joins in.

Nick "See. How cool does that look?
The moat looks awesome. And those
towers you made at the front look
so real."

Matt "Yes, not bad if I do say
so myself."

The boys stand back and proudly look over their sensational sand creation. Meanwhile an older boy appears and heads towards them. He sneers at Nick and Matt then suddenly kicks the castle over.

CHAPTER 3

Vanilla and Bury

The older boy laughs loudly as he
trudges off from Matt and Nick's
destroyed sandcastle.

Nick "I can't believe he just did
   that. We've got to do something!"
Matt "Yeah, like what? Go up to
   him and tell him to say sorry—not!
   You saw how big he was."

Nick "Well, what about our castle?"

Matt "Just forget it, let's do something else."

Nick "Like what?"

Matt "Bury me!"

Nick "What? Completely?"

Matt "No! Just up to my neck."

Nick "Okay!"

Matt and Nick begin to dig a large trench in the sand, while their dads watch on nearby.

Nick "Right, get in."

Matt lies in the trench while Nick covers him with sand.

Matt "Cool, I can't move."
Nick "It's weird just seeing your head sticking out like that."
Matt "It feels good. Hey, is that your mum calling?"

Nick "Yes, and yours is calling too. I'll go and see what they want."

Nick returns licking an ice-cream to where Matt is buried.

Matt "Awwh, is that chocolate and vanilla?"

Nick "Yes, and it's delicious. Mmm!"

Matt "Get me out of here! I want some ice-cream too!"

Nick "No. Mmm, mmm. This
ice-cream is the best in the world!
Mmmmm!"

Matt "Nick! Get this sand off me!"

Nick continues to tease Matt. He
kneels beside his head and waves
the ice-cream in front of him.

Nick "Do you want a lick?"

Matt "No, I want my own. Help me out of this hole NOW!"

Nick "Forget it then. No lick, no freedom."

Matt "Okay, okay! I want a lick!"

As Nick moves his ice-cream closer to Matt's mouth, the ice-cream scoop suddenly drops from its cone right on top of Matt's face.

CHAPTER 4

Shark Attack?

Nick tries to wipe the ice-cream off Matt's face. But as he does he gets sand in the ice-cream and spoils it completely. He eventually digs Matt out of the ground.

Matt "*Now* how's your ice-cream! Serves you right for teasing me, you loser."

Nick "I shouldn't have tried to give you some."

Matt "Well, let's get some more."

The boys dash over to their families and they each have an ice-cream. Twenty minutes later Matt and Nick are back in the water again, trying to ride some more waves.

Matt "These waves are all too small. We have to wait for a bigger set."

Nick "What was that?"

Matt "What was what?"

Nick "Something just touched my leg."

Matt "As if. You're just imagining things."

Nick "Seriously, I felt something. You don't think it was a shark, do you?"

Matt "If it was, you wouldn't be talking to me now."

Nick "Yes, I guess so. Do you think there are any sharks swimming around now?"

Matt "Yes! We're in an ocean.
They're everywhere. We're in
their home."

Nick "Well, aren't you worried?"

Matt "No, because if I saw a shark I
would do a karate chop on its nose
and make it cry like a baby!"

Nick "So, you're telling me you're not
scared of a huge man-eating, killing
shark chomping your guts out?"

Matt "No."

Nick "Then what's that out there?"

Matt turns to see a large grey
shadow just beneath the surface in
the distance.

Matt "Oh no! It's a shark! We've got
to get out of here!"
Nick "I thought you said you
weren't scared!"
Matt "Are you nuts? I was joking!
Swim for it!"

CHAPTER 5

Cheeky Surf

Matt and Nick frantically swim for their lives. That is, until Nick looks back and realises that there isn't a shark after all. He grabs hold of Matt's foot.

Nick "Stop!"
Matt "What?"
Nick "Look!"

The grey shadow rises to the surface. A man wearing a snorkel and flippers swims past.

Matt "A snorkeller?"

Nick "Looks like it. Phew! That was lucky. I thought we were dead meat."

Matt "I didn't. I really wasn't that scared ... really."

Nick "Oh yes? You were swimming so fast you could've won an Olympic gold medal."

Matt "I suppose so. Look!"

Nick turns and spots a huge wave heading their way.

Nick "That's bigger than the one I caught!"

Matt "I know. We have to get it."

Nick "Yes. And it looks like *he's* going to try to catch it too."

Nick and Matt glance across to see it's the older boy who kicked over their castle.

Matt "Well, I hope he misses it. Okay, are you ready? Here it comes!"

Nick "Let's go for it!"

Matt and Nick swim like crazy and together they successfully ride the enormous wave all the way to the beach.

Nick and Matt "YEAHHHHH!!!!"

The boys pick themselves up and give each other a high-five slap. They then realise the older boy has missed the wave completely. They also notice that he is missing something else— his swimming trunks.

Nick (chuckling) "Look, his trunks came off!"

Matt grabs the boy's trunks out of the water. The boy calls out: "Hey, give me back my swimming trunks."

Matt "That's what you get for kicking down other people's castles!"

Nick "What are we going to do with
them? He looks really embarrassed.
How's he going to come out of the
water now?"

Matt "I've got an idea!"

Minutes later Matt and Nick have
built another sandcastle with a flag
on top using a stick and a ... stray
pair of trunks!

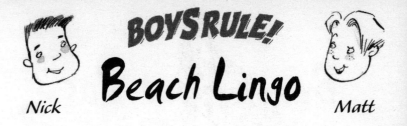

body surf When you ride a wave without using a surf board.

ice-cream A smooth, sweet, cold food made from frozen dairy products and flavouring. Also a great teaser to dangle in front of your friends buried in sand!

shore The land along the edge of a sea, ocean, lake or coast.

sunscreen A skin lotion or cream which protects you from being burnt by the sun's rays.

tsunami A humungous wave caused by an earthquake.

Beach Must-dos

☞ Always wear sunscreen with a sun protection factor (SPF) of at least 15, even on cloudy days. You don't want to get fried.

☞ Make sure your trunks are on tightly enough or they could come off in the surf.

☞ Insist to your parents that you must have an ice-cream. It always tastes better at the beach.

☞ Drink plenty of fresh water, but not salt water—it just makes you thirstier!

☞ Get out of the water ... fast! ... if you see any sort of grey fin swimming by.

☞ Always swim between the lifesavers' flags—they show you the safest place to swim.

☞ Build a sandcastle—it's not as babyish as you might think. Wet sand works best.

☞ Wear flip flops or sandals if the sand is too hot.

☞ Never swim by yourself—it's no fun and it's not safe.

Beach Instant Info

The longest sand sculpture ever built was 26 375 metres in length. It was built by more than 10 000 people at Myrtle Beach, South Carolina, USA in 1991.

One of the largest surf companies in the world is Quiksilver.

One of the world's most successful surf companies is Billabong.

Brazil is known for producing not only the best soccer players in the world but also the best beach volleyball players.

The oldest human footprints were discovered on a rocky shore in South Africa.

The largest beach towel in the world was made in Spain. It's 9.4 metres wide by 14.5 metres long.

Australian Kelly Slater is one of the most famous surfers in the world.

Devon and Cornwall have some of the most popular beaches for holidays.

Think Tank

1 What should you wear to protect yourself from the sun's harmful rays?

2 What's a short name for swimming trunks?

3 Is a dolphin a fish?

4 What's the term for surfing without a board?

5 What's an ocean of the world that starts with the letter "P"?

6 What sort of bird are you likely to see at the beach?

7 What are you supposed to swim between at the beach?

8 What's a sandcastle made out of?

Answers

How did you score?

- If you got all 8 answers correct, you definitely love going to the beach. You'd go every day if you could.

- If you got 6 answers correct, you love the beach but sometimes can't stand all the sand getting all over you.

- If you scored fewer than 4 answers, then you probably like looking at the sea, rather than being in it. But you'd still eat ice-cream at the beach.

Felice → ← Phil

Hi Guys!

We have heaps of fun reading and want you to, too. We both believe that being a good reader is really important and so cool.

Try out our suggestions to help you have fun as you read.

At school, why don't you use "Hit the Beach" as a play and you and your friends can be the actors. Set the scene for your play. Bring some beach gear to school to use as props but maybe leave the sand at the beach! If you haven't got a bucket and spade, use your acting skills and imagination to pretend.

So ... have you decided who is going to be Nick and who is going to be Matt? Now, with your friends, read and act out our story in front of the class.

We have a lot of fun when we go to schools and read our stories. After we finish the kids all clap really loudly. When you've finished your play your classmates will do the same. Just remember to look out the window—there might be a talent scout from a television station watching you!

Reading at home is really important and a lot of fun as well.

Take our books home and get someone in your family to read them with you. Maybe they can take on a part in the story.

Remember, reading is a whole lot of fun.

So, as the frog in the local pond would say, Read-it!

And remember, Boys Rule!

BOYS RULE!
When We Were Kids

Felice

Phil

Felice "Did you ever go to the beach when you were young?"

Phil "All the time! Did you?"

Felice "I used to visit a beach called Squeaky Beach because the sand was so clean and white it would squeak when you walked on it."

Phil "Cool. I used to visit a beach called Ow Beach."

Felice "You mean Owl Beach?"

Phil "No, Ow. Actually, its real name was Sunset Beach but everyone called it Ow Beach because the sand was so hot that you'd scream 'ow! ow! ow!' with every step you took!"

What a Laugh!

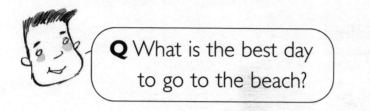

Q What is the best day to go to the beach?

A SUN-day!

BOYS RULE!

Gone Fishing	The Tree House	Golf Legends	Camping Out	Bike Daredevils
Water Rats	Skateboard Dudes	Tennis Ace	Basketball Buddies	Secret Agent Heroes
Wet World	Rock Star	Pirate Attack	Olympic Champions	Race Car Dreamers
Hit the Beach	Rotten School Day	Halloween Gotcha!	Battle of the Games	On the Farm